Sp

SPURGEON'S VERSE EXPOSITION OF

By Charles H. Spurgeon

ISBN: 9781520920658

March 2017

Charles H. Spurgeon's 1st John Commentary Contents

FOREWORD

Charles Haddon Spurgeon (1834-92) is known as the Prince of Preachers because of his extraordinary gift as a preacher of God's word. His ability was God-given and he used it for the glory of his Lord.

He gave his heart and life to Christ at the age of 15 after being forced to seek shelter from a snow storm in a Methodist chapel. Spurgeon was only 19 when he was called into full-time ministry as pastor of New Park Street Chapel. This Church, of course, eventually grew through God's grace which necessitated it moving to newly built premises and took the new name of the Metropolitan Tabernacle.

Spurgeon is most often remembered as being a preacher with little emphasis placed on other areas of his ministry. He was responsible for facilitating the opening of an orphanage, a college for training pastors and greatly supported the selling of Christian books. His ministry was anything but one-sided!

What we should remember is that Spurgeon communicated God's word and he was happy to use any medium that was available to him. His written works were invaluable as they were available to the many people who were unable to hear him preach. Indeed his volume, "Lectures To My Students" was published and as well as general sale copies were provided to many ministers around the country at their request and at the expense of Susannah Spurgeon who administered a fund to facilitate this generosity.

This book you are holding is not the product of Spurgeon's writing ministry nor the result of his preaching. These words are all Spurgeon's and they came about as the result of him expounding a chapter of the Bible during his Sunday service. Such was his gift that he could do this with very little specific preparation. He would select a chapter and tell the congregation the salient points and matters contained therein.

It is not a complete commentary of Scripture, indeed many chapters of the Bible did not receive this attention from him. Indeed in this commentary on Ephesians he had not provided an exegesis on chapter 4. But what Spurgeon left was a legacy of inspired, accurate and valuable insights into Scripture. These words you will read are for the preacher but, and more importantly, they are for every Christian. We pray that you will find that they help open Scripture to you in a new way.

We make use of commentaries, lexicons and concordances to help us better understand God's word. But these tools must never supplant or replace the Bible.

There is no substitute to reading His word in order that we might apply it to our own lives.

Every blessing in the name of our Lord, Jesus Christ.

SPURGEON 1 JOHN 1

Verses 1-3

1 John 1:1. That which was from, the beginning, which we have heard, which we have seen with our eyes, which we have looked upon, and our hands have handled of the Word of life;

The fact that Christ was really in the flesh, that he was no phantom, no shadow mocking the eyes that looked upon him, is exceedingly important, and hence John (whose style, by the way, in this Epistle is precisely like the style which he uses in his Gospel) — John begins by declaring that Jesus Christ, the Son of God, who in his eternity was from the beginning, was really a substantial man, for he says, “We have heard him” — hearing is good evidence; “Which we have seen with our eyes” — eyesight is good, clear evidence certainly; “Which we have locked upon” — this is better still, for this imports a deliberate, careful, circumspect gaze; but better still, “Which our hands have handled” — for John had leaned his head on Jesus Christ’s bosom, and his hands had often met the real flesh and blood of the living Saviour. We need have no doubt about the reality of Christ’s incarnation when we have these open eyes and hands to give us evidence.

1 John 1:2. For the life was manifested, and we have seen it, and bear witness, and shew unto you, that eternal life, which was with the Father, and was manifested unto us;

That same eternal Being who is Very God of Very God, and is worthy to be called essentially Life, was made flesh and, dwelt among us, and the apostles could say, “We beheld his glory.”

1 John 1:3. That which we have sees and heard declare we unto you,

See how he does hammer this nail as if he will drive it fast! How he rings this bell that it may toll the death-knell of every doubt!

1 John 1:3. That ye also may have fellowship with us:

But John, what is the value of fellowship with you, you and your brethren, a parcel of poor fishermen; who warts fellows with you — hooted, despised, mocked, and persecuted in every city — who wants fellowship with you?

1 John 1:3. And truly our fellowship is with the Father, and with his Son Jesus Christ.

What a leap from the fisherman to the Father's throne, from the poor, despised son of Zebedee up to the King of Kings! Oh! John, we would have fellowship with thee now T We will have fellowship with thy scorn and spitting, that we may have fellowship with thee, and with the Father, and his Son, Jesus Christ.

This exposition consisted of readings from Genesis 24:1-16; 1 Samuel 30:1-13; 1 John 1:1-3.

Verses 1-10

1 John 1:1. That which was from the beginning, which we have heard, which we have seen with our eyes, which we have looked upon, and our hands have handled, of the Word of life;

The fact that Christ was really in the flesh, that he was no phantom, no shadow mocking the eyes that looked upon him, is exceedingly important, and hence John-(whose style, by the way, in this epistle is precisely like the style which he uses in his Gospel)-John begins by declaring that Jesus Christ, the Son of God, who in his eternity was from the beginning, was really a substantial man, for he says-" We have heard him "-hearing is good evidence, " Which we have seen him with our own eyes; " eye-sight is good, clear evidence, certainly, " Which we have looked upon "- this is better still, for this imports a deliberate, careful, circumspect gaze; but better still- "which our hands have handled," for John had leaned his head on Jesus Christ's bosom, and his hands had often met the real flesh and blood of the living Saviour. We need have no doubt about the reality of Christ's incarnation when we have these open eyes and hands to give us evidence.

1 John 1:2. (For the life was manifested, and we have seen it, and bear witness, and shew unto you that eternal life, which was with the Father, and was manifested unto us;)

That same eternal Being who is Very God of Very God, and is worthy to be called essentially Life, was made flesh and dwelt among us, and the Apostles could say-" We beheld his glory."

1 John 1:3. That which we have seen and heard declare we unto you-

See how he does hammer this nail as if he will drive it fast! How he rings this bell that it may toll the death-knell of every doubt!

1 John 1:3. That which we have seen and heard declare we unto you, that ye also may have fellowship with us:

But John, what is the value of fellowship with you, you and your brethren, a parcel of poor fishermen, who wants fellowship with you-hooted, despised, mocked and persecuted in every city-who wants fellowship with you?

1 John 1:3. And truly our fellowship is with the Father, and with trio Son Jesus Christ.

What a leap from the fisherman to the Father's throne, from the poor, despised son of Zebedee up to the King of Kings! Oh, John, we would have fellowship with thee now! We will have fellowship with thy scorn and spitting, that we may have fellowship with thee, and with the Father, and his Son Jesus Christ.

1 John 1:4. And these things write I unto you that your joy may be full.

Some Christians have joy, but there are only a few drops in the bottom of their cup; but the Scriptures were written, and more especially the doctrine of an Incarnate God is revealed to us, that our joy may be full. Why, if you have nothing else to make you glad the feet that Jesus has become brother to you, arrayed in your flesh, should make your joy full.

1 John 1:5. This then is the message which we have heard of him, and declare unto you, that God is light, and in him is no darkness at all.

Not a light, nor the light, though he is both, but that he is light. Scripture uses the term light for knowledge, for purity, for prosperity, for happiness, and for truth. God is light, and then in his usual style, John, who not only tells you a truth but always guards it, adds-" in whom is no darkness at all."

1 John 1:6. If we say that we have fellowship with him, and walk in darkness, we lie, and do not the truth.

Mark here, this does not mean walking in the darkness of sorrow, for there are many of God's people that walk in the darkness of doubts and fears, and yet they have fellowship with God; nay, they sometimes have fellowship with Christ all the better for the darkness of the path along which they walk, but the darkness here meant is the darkness of sin, the darkness of untruthfulness. If I walk in a lie, or walk in sin, and then profess to have fellowship with God, I have lied, and do not the truth.

1 John 1:7. But if we walk in the light, as he is in the light,-

Not to the same degree, but in the same manner-
7.We have fellowship one with another, and the blood of Jesus Christ his Son cleanseth us from all sin.

So you see that when we walk the best, when we walk in the light, as he is in the light, when our fellowship is of the highest order, yet still we want daily cleansing. It does not say-mark this O my soul-it does not say " The blood of Jesus Christ cleansed " but " cleanseth." If guilt return, his power may be proved again and again, there is no fear that all my daily slips and shortcomings shall be graciously removed by this precious blood. But there are some who think they are perfectly sanctified and have no sin.

1 John 1:8-9. If we say that we have no sin, we deceive ourselves, and the truth is not in us. If we confess our sins, he is faithful and just to forgive us our sins, and to cleanse us from all unrighteousness.

Oh, those words, and more especially that glorious word " all! " This must include the vilest sin that ever stained human nature, the blackest grime that ever came from the black heart of man. And now John is very careful when he strikes a blow to hit completely. He has already smitten those who say they have no sin, and now he smites those who say they did not at one time have any.

1 John 1:10. If we say that we have not sinned, we make him a liar, and his word is not in us.

This exposition consisted of readings from Psalms 130:1-8; 1 John 1:1-10; 1 John 2:1-2.

Verses 4-7

1 John 1:4. And these things write we unto you, that your joy may be full.

Some Christians have joy, but there are only a few drops in the bottom of their cup; but the Scriptures were written, and more especially the doctrine of an Incarnate God is revealed to us that our joy may be full. Why, if you have nothing else to make you glad, the fact that Jesus has become brother to you, arrayed in your flesh, should make your joy full.

1 John 1:5. This then is the message which we have heard of him, and declare unto you, that God is light, and in him is no darkness at all.

Not a light, nor the light, though he is both, but that he is light. Scripture uses the term light for knowledge, for purity, for prosperity, for happiness, and for truth. God is light, and then in his usual style John, who not only bells you a truth, but always guards it, adds, “in whom is no darkness at all.”

1 John 1:6. If we say that we have fellowship with him, and walk in darkness, we lie, and do not the truth.

Mark here, this does not mean walking in the darkness of sorrow, for there are many of God’s people that walk in the darkness of doubts and fears, and yet they have fellowship with God; nay, they sometimes have fellowship with Christ all the better for the darkness of the path along which they walk; but the darkness here meant is the darkness of sin, the darkness of untruthfulness. If I walk in a lie, or walk in sin, and then profess to have fellowship with God, I have lied, and do not the truth.

1 John 1:7. But if we walk in the light as he is in the light,

Not to the same degree, but in the same manner.

1 John 1:7. We have fellowship one with another, and the blood of Jesus Christ his Son cleanseth us from all sin.

So you see that when we walk the best, when we walk in the light as he is in the light, when our fellowship is of the highest order, yet still we want daily cleansing. It does not say — mark this, O my soul — it does not. If say, The blood of Jesus Christ “cleansed,” but “cleanseth.” guilt return, his power may be proved again and again; there is no fear that all my daily slips and shortcomings shall be graciously removed by this precious blood. But there are some who think they are perfectly sanctified and have no sin.

This exposition consisted of readings from Psalms 130; 1 John 1:4-7.

SPURGEON 1 JOHN 2

Verse 1

1 John 2:1. My little children, these things I write unto you, that ye sin not.

This is one of the great objects of all that is written by inspiration, — that we may be kept from sin. O child of God, as thou wouldst fear to drink poison, as thou wouldst flee from a serpent, dread sin!

1 John 2:1. And if any man sin, —

Is it a hopeless case then? Far from it: "If any man sin," —

1 John 2:1-3. We have an advocate with the Father, Jesus Christ the righteous, and he is the propitiation for our sins: and not for our's only, but also for the sins of the whole world. And hereby we do know that we know him, if we keep his commandments.

Holiness of life is the best proof that we know God. It matters not how readily we can speak about God, nor how much we suppose that we love him, the great test is, do we keep his commandments? What a heart-searching test this is! How it should humble us before the mercy-seat!

1 John 2:4-6. He that saith, I know him, and keepeth not his commandment, is a liar and the truth is not in him. But whoso keepeth his word, in him verily is the love of God perfected: hereby know we that we are in him. He that saith he abideth in him ought himself also so to walk, even as he walked.

When we try to be, in every respect, what God's Word tells us we ought to be, then may we know that we are in God; but if we walk carelessly, if we take no account of our actions, but do, after a random fashion, whatever comes into our foolish hearts, then have we no evidence at all that we are in God.

1 John 2:7. Brethren, I write no new commandment unto you, but an old commandment which ye had from the beginning.

The old commandment is the word which ye have heard from the beginning. "From the time when Christ first began to preach, or when the gospel was first preached in your ears."

1 John 2:8. Again, a new commandment I write unto you, which thing is true in him and in you: because the darkness is past, and the true light now shineth.

That which is new in the gospel, in one sense, is not new in another; for, though John was about to write what he called a new commandment, yet, at the same time, he was writing something which was not novel, something which was not grafted upon the gospel, but which grows naturally out of it, namely, the law of love.

1 John 2:9. He that saith he is in the light, and hateth his brother, is in darkness, even until now.

God is love, and God is light therefore, love is light, and the light of God is love. Where enmity and hatred are “till in the heart, it is proof positive that the grace of God is not there.

1 John 2:10-15. He that loveth his brother abideth in the light, and there is none occasion of stumbling in him. But he that hateth his brother is in darkness, and walketh in darkness, and knoweth not whither he goeth, because that darkness hath blinded his eyes. I write unto you, little children, because your sins are forgiven you for his name’s sake. I write unto you, fathers, because ye have known him that is from the beginning. I write unto you, young men, because ye have overcome the wicked one. I write unto you, little children, because ye have known the Father. I have written unto you, fathers, because ye have known him that is from the beginning. I have written unto you, young men, because ye are strong, and the word of God abideth in you, and ye have overcome the wicked one. Love not the world, neither the things that are in the world. If any man love the world, the love of the Father is not in him.

For this sinful world is directly opposed to the Father. You cannot send your heart at the same time in two opposite ways, — towards evil and towards good; you must make a choice between the two.

1 John 2:16-17. For all that is in the world, the best of the flesh, and the lust of the eyes, and the pride of life, is not of the Father, but is of the world. And the world passeth away, and the lust thereof: but he that doeth the will of God abideth for ever. It ought not, then, to be difficult to make a choice between these fleeting shadows and the everlasting substance.

1 John 2:18. Little children, it is the last time: —

You may read the passage, “It is the last hour,” as if John wanted to show how late it was, and how soon Christ would come: “It is the last hour:” —

1 John 2:18. And as ye have heard that antichrist shall come, even now are there many antichrists; whereby we know that it is the last time.

How much more emphatically John might write this verse if he were writing today!

1 John 2:19. They went out from us, —

For, alas! many of the antichrists came out of the church; they sprang up from among the followers of Christ: "They went out from us," —

1 John 2:19-20. But they were not of us; for if they had been of us, they would no doubt have continued with us but they went out, that they might be made manifest that they were not all of us. But ye have an unction from the Holy One, and ye know all things.

"You who know God — and even the little children, the babes in Christ, know the Father, — know all "things; and you will not be led astray and deceived by these antichrists who have gone out into the world"

1 John 2:21. I have not written unto you because ye know not the truth, but because ye know it, and that no lie is of the truth.

The truth is all of a piece, and a lie cannot be a part of the truth. Christ does not teach us a Jesuitical system in which error and falsehood are mixed up with truth; the gospel is all truth, and to those who believe it we may say, "Ye know the truth, and ye also know that no lie is of the truth."

1 John 2:22-23. Who is a liar but he that denieth that Jesus is the Christ? He is antichrist, that denieth the Father and the Son. Whoever denieth the Son, the same hath not the Father: —

They who deny the Deity of Christ practically deny the Divine Fatherhood of God. It is not possible for us to understand the rest of truth if we do not believe in Christ, who is the Truth. As the poet says, — "You cannot be right in the rest Unless you think rightly of him."

1 John 2:23-28. [But] he that acknowledgeth the son hath the Father also. Let that therefore abide in you, which ye have heard from the beginning. If that which ye have heard from the beginning shall remain in you, ye also shall continue in the Son, and in the Father. And that is the promise that he hath promised us, even eternal life. These things have I written unto you concerning them that seduce you. But the anointing which ye have received of him abideth in you, and ye need not that any man teach you: but as the same anointing teacheth you of all things, and in truth, and is no lie, and even as it hath taught you, we shall abide in him. And now, little children, abide in him; —

That which is the subject of promise is also the subject of precept; and the precepts of the gospel are given to Christians because, in this way, God keeps his own promise, and so leads me to obey his precepts.

1 John 2:28-29. That, when he shall appear, we may have confidence, and not be ashamed before him at his coming. If ye know that he is righteous, ye know that every one that doeth righteousness is born of him.

1 John 3:1-2. Behold, what manner of love the Father hath bestowed upon us, that we should be called the sons of God: therefore the world knoweth us not, because it knew him not. Beloved, now are we the sons of God, and it doth not yet appear what we shall be: but we know that, when he shall appear, we shall be like him; for we shall see him as he is.

Verse 1-2

1 John 2:1. My little children, these things write I unto you, that ye sin not.

He is anxious that they should not sin, he knows they do, and that if they say they do not, they lie. Still the Christian's object is sinless perfection, and though he will never have it till he gets to heaven, that is all the better because he will always then be pressing forward, and never reckoning that he has attained.

1 John 2:1-2. And if any man sin, we have an advocate with the Father, Jesus Christ the righteous. And he is the propitiation for our sins: and not for ours only, but also for the sins of the whole world.

By which is meant, not only that Jesus Christ died for Gentiles as well as Jews, and for some of all nations, but that there is that in the atonement of Christ which might be sufficient for every creature under heaven if God had so chosen every creature, the limitation lying, not in the value of the atonement itself, but in the design and intention of the Eternal God. God sent his Son to lay down his life for his sheep. We know that Christ redeemed us from among men, so that the redemption is particularly and specially for the elect; yet at the same time the price offered was so precious the blood was so infinite in value, that if every man that ever lived had to be redeemed Christ could have done it. It is this that make us bold to preach the Gospel to every creature, since we know there is no limit in the value of the atonement, though still we know that the design of it is for the chosen people of God alone.

This exposition consisted of readings from Psalms 130:1-8; 1 John 1:1-10; 1 John 2:1-2.

Verses 1-6

1 John 2:1. My little children, these things write I unto you, that ye sin not.

That you may abstain from it, and abhor it, and not indulge in anything that would lead you towards it.

1 John 2:1. And if any man sin, we have an advocate with the Father, Jesus Christ the righteous:

We are to seek to live a perfectly holy life, but inasmuch as we constantly fall short of that ideal, here is our comfort; we still have an Advocate, we still have One who undertakes our cause, and pleads for us before his Father's throne.

1 John 2:2. And he is the propitiation for our sins: and not for our's only, but also for the sins of the whole world.

Whoever comes to him shall receive deliverance from sin. Neither Jew nor Gentile is exclusively considered in the offering of the atonement of Christ; those for whom he died are of every race, and color, and class, and kin.

1 John 2:3-6. And hereby we do know that we know him, if we keep his commandments. He that saith, I know him, and keepeth not his commandments, is a liar, and the truth is not in him. But whoso keepeth his word, in him verily is the love of God perfected: hereby know we that we are in him. He that saith he abideth in him ought himself also so to walk, even as he walked.

May the Holy Spirit graciously lead us all to this extraordinary walk of grace, for our Lord Jesus Christ's sake! Amen.

This exposition consisted of readings from 1 John 1 and 1 John 2:1-6.

Verses 1-29

1 John 2:1. My little children, these things write I unto you, that ye sin not.

For this we ought to watch and strive, that we sin not.

1 John 2:1. And if any man sin-

What then? Is it a hopeless case? Oh, no, far from it; it is a sad case, but there is a remedy for it: " and if any man sin,"-

1 John 2:1-2. We have an advocate with the Father, Jesus Christ the righteous: and he is the propitiation for our sins: and not for ours only, but also for the sins of the whole world.

Come ye, then, to Christ for pardon, whether ye are Jews or Gentiles, whether ye are saints or sinners, whether ye are old or young, whether ye are moral or immoral, for God is both able and willing to forgive all manner of sin because of the propitiation offered by his well-beloved Son " Jesus Christ the righteous."

1 John 2:3. And hereby we do know that we know him, if we keep his commandments.

Obedience is the test of discipleship. Mere head knowledge is all in vain, and all in vain our fears, unless we render a practical obedience to the commandments of Christ. We shall not only savingly know him, but we shall " know that we know him, if we keep his commandments."

1 John 2:4. He that saith, I know him, and keepeth not his commandments, is a liar and the truth is not in him.

This is a terrible condition for anyone to be in, to say that he knows Christ, and yet to have the Holy Spirit calling him a liar because he is not keeping Christ's commandments. Again I remind you that obedience is essential to Christian discipleship. If we refuse to obey Christ's commandments it is clear that we do not really know the Saviour at all, we are not even beginners in the school of Christ.

1 John 2:5. But whoso keepeth his word, in him verily is the love of God perfected: hereby know we that we are in him.

When every word of his is precious to us and when we strive to live according to his precepts, then we know that "we are in him." This is even more than knowing that we know him, for it is the assurance that we are united to him by a living connection which can never be broken.

1 John 2:6. He that saith he abideth in him ought himself also so to walk, even as he walked.

What a walk would that be! How holy, harmless, undefiled, and separate from sinners is the man who tries to walk even as Christ walked.

" Lord, I desire to live as one Who bears a blood-bought name,
As one who fears but grieving thee,
And knows no other shame."
" As one by whom thy walk below Should never be forgot.
As one who fain would keep apart From all thou lovest not."

1 John 2:7-9. Brethren, I write no new commandment unto you, but an old commandment which ye had from the beginning. The old commandment is the word which ye have heard from the beginning. Again, a new commandment I write unto you, which thing is true in him and in you: because the darkness is past, and the true light now shineth. He that saith he is in the light, and hateth his brother, is in darkness even until now.

Love is the true test of light, that light which leads us to love God, to love Christ, to love the truth, to love God's people, ay, and to love the whole world of men for their good, this is the love that attests the light we have to be the very light of God.

1 John 2:10. He that loveth his brother abideth in the light, and there is none occasion of stumbling in him.

A loving spirit, kind, generous, forgiving, unselfish, seeking the good of others,-this is one of the best proofs that our natural darkness has gone, and that true spiritual light is within us. Some persons think very much of the doctrine of Christ, but very little of the Spirit of Christ. Let such remember that it is written, "If any man have not the Spirit of Christ, he is none of his." If we do not know what it is to love, then we do not in the Scriptural sense know what it is to live, we are dead. Hatred is the cerement in which the dead soul is wound up, the grave clothes in which it is put away in the tomb; but love is the garment of life in which a truly quickened spirit arrays itself. The one who is full of hatred dwells in darkness, but he that loveth abideth in the light. Note how love and life and light are most blessedly linked to one another.

1 John 2:11-13. But he that hateth his brother is in darkness, and walketh in darkness, and knoweth not whither he goeth, because that darkness hath blinded his eyes. I write unto you, little children, because your sins are forgiven you, for his name's sake. I write unto you, fathers, because ye have known him that is from the beginning.

"You are old men, and you like to think of old things. The everlasting love of God, the covenant made with Christ before the worlds were formed these are things that are very dear to you; and you prize beyond all other; 'him that is from the beginning."'

1 John 2:13. I write unto you, young men, because ye have overcome the wicked one.

"In the days of your strength, you have won the victory which no human power can ever win unaided. You have overcome that wicked one who would easily have overcome you if you had been left to fight him by yourselves. "

1 John 2:13. I write unto you, little children, because ye have known the Father.

That is all that little children need to know at first. They may not know the great mysteries that the fathers have fathomed, they may not well know some things that the young men know, but even babes in Christ know the Father, and rejoice in his love.

1 John 2:14. I have written unto you, fathers, because ye have known him that is from the beginning.

Twice, you see, John says the same thing about the fathers, and he says nothing more concerning them; but truly to "have known him that is from the beginning is practically to know all that even the fathers need to know or can know, for this knowledge includes all other that is worth knowing.

1 John 2:14. I have written unto you, young men, because ye are strong, and the word of God abideth in you, and ye have overcome the wicked one.

Here again John repeats his former statement concerning the young men, but he adds to it "because ye are strong and the word of God abideth in you." There is a purpose in the repetition of each case, it is to emphasize the importance of the apostolic declarations.

1 John 2:15. Love not the world, neither the things that are in the world.

"Your affections are meant for something better than these transient and defiled things; so let not your heart's love flow out to things so soiled and base. 'Set your affection on things above, not on things on the earth.'"

1 John 2:15. If any man love the world, the love of the Father is not in him.

These two things are such deadly opposites that they cannot live together where the love of the father is, there cannot be the love of the world. There is no room in us for two loves. The love of the world is essentially idolatry, and God will not be worshipped side by side with idols. "If any man love the world, the love of the Father is not in him." Does not that text draw a very sharp distinction between those who love the Lord, and those who love him not? Remember children of God, that this is the language of John, the apostle of love; but true love is honest, outspoken, heart-searching, heart-trying. Do not imagine that there is any love to your souls in the heart of the preacher who preaches smooth things, and who flatters you with his "Peace, peace," when there is no peace. No, the highest, deepest, most heaven-inspired love is that which searches and tries the heart felt there should be any deception there.

1 John 2:16. For all that is in the world, the lust of the flesh, and the lust of the eyes, and the pride of life, is not of the Father, but is of the world.

That devil's trinity-" the lust of the flesh, and the lust of the eyes, and the pride of life,"-"is not of the Father, but is of the world."

1 John 2:17. And the world passeth away, and the lust thereof:

It is only a puff, a phantom, a bubble, a mirage which will melt away as you try to approach it; there is nothing substantial in it.

1 John 2:17. But he that doeth the will of God abideth for ever.

Not, "he that doeth some great thing to be seen of men, " not, " he that builds a row of almshouses, or leaves a great mass of money to charity when he dies, because he could not possibly carry it away with him, "not, "he that sounds a trumpet before him to let everybody know what a good man he is;" not, "he that must needs outdistance everybody else;" but, "he that doeth the will of God abideth for ever." Obedience to the will of God is the pathway to perpetual honour and everlasting joy.

1 John 2:18. Little children, it is the last time: and as ye have heard that antichrist shall come, even now are there many antichrists; whereby we know that it is the last time.

And now, I think, even more than when John wrote, is this the fact for antichrists are multiplying on all sides, and there are even worse evils to come than we have seen as yet; and it therefore behooves Christians to be upon the watch and to let this truth comfort them, that "it is the last time." Once get through this dispensation, and the battle is ended; even though the dispensation should be protracted beyond our hope and desire, yet, still, once get through it, and it is over. This is to be the last charge of our great adversary and all his hosts. Stand fast, therefore, ye soldiers of the Cross, stand like rocks amidst the onslaught of the waves, and the victory shall yet be yours.

1 John 2:19. They went out from us, but they were not of us: for if they had been of us, they would no doubt have continued with us: but they went out, that they might be made manifest that they were not all of us.

The worst of men go out from among the best of men, the antichrists go out from the church of Christ. The raw material for a devil was an angel. To make a Judas, you must make him out of an apostle. May God purify his professing church since even in her own loins she breeds adversaries of the faith.

1 John 2:20. But ye have an unction from the Holy One, and ye know all things.

The Spirit of God will teach you as you need to know. He will so instruct you that you shall know all that is for your soul's good, and for his own glory.

1 John 2:21. I have not written unto you because ye know not the truth, but because ye know it, and that no lie is of the truth.

That which is of man's making is false, "but the word of the Lord endureth for ever. And this is the word which by the gospel is preached unto you."

1 John 2:22-23. Who is a liar but he that denieth that Jesus is the Christ. He is antichrist, that denieth the Father and the Son. Whosoever denieth the Son the same hath not the Father: [but] he that acknowledgeth the Son hath the Father also.

Some pretend to honour the Father while they dishonour the Son, but this can never really be done. Jesus truly said, " I and my Father are one," so that he that denieth the Son denieth the Father also.

1 John 2:24. Let that therefore abide in you, which ye have heard from the beginning. If that which ye have heard from the beginning shall remain in you, ye also shall, continue in the Son, and in the Father.

As it was the truth that was revealed to them at the first, there was no need of a later revelation to correct the mistakes of the first, as some foolishly and falsely teach nowadays.

1 John 2:25. And this is the promise that he hath promised us, even eternal life.

Let those that want them have these novelties, these constant changes we who believe in Jesus have something far better, even the promise of eternal life.

1 John 2:26. These things have I written unto you concerning them that seduce you.

They would lead you astray if they could so beware of them. " Forewarned is forearmed."

1 John 2:27-28. But the anointing which ye have received of him abideth in you, and ye need not that any man teach you: but as the same anointing teacheth you of all things, and is truth, and is no lie, and even as it hath taught you, ye shall abide in him. And now, little children, abide in him;-How John continues to urge us to stand fast in Christ. As the Holy Ghost has taught us to trust Christ, so would he have us " abide in him."

And this is one great reason why we are to abide in him;"-

1 John 2:28-29. That, when he shall appear, we may have confidence, and not be ashamed before him at his coming. If ye know that he is righteous, ye know that every one that doeth righteousness is born of him.

SPURGEON 1 JOHN 3

Verses 1-24

1 John 3:1. Behold, what manner of love the Father hath bestowed upon us, that we should be called the sons of God:

Behold it, wonder at it, and never cease to admire it. Is it not one of the greatest marvels that even God himself has ever wrought that we should be called the sons of God?

1 John 3:1. Therefore the world knoweth us not, because it knew him not.

It does not know the Father, then how should it know the children? It did not know the elder Brother, — the firstborn among many brethren, — and as it did not know him, how should it know us?

1 John 3:2. Beloved, now are we the sons of God, and it doth not yet appear what we shall be: but we know that, when he shall appear, we shall be like him; for we shall see him as he is.

And that vision will be transforming and transfiguring. The pure in heart see God, and they are pure because they see God. There is both action and reaction, when God has purified us we shall see Christ and when we see Christ as he is, our purification will be complete. When will that day arrive? Oh, for the blessed vision! Meanwhile, let us be content to look at him by faith, and to be ever growing more and more prepared for that brighter vision which is yet to be ours.

1 John 3:3. And every man that hath this hope in him purifies himself, even as he is pure.

It is the nature of this divine hope, — this hope of being like Christ — that it helps us to grow day by day more like him; and so we purify ourselves, as Christ is pure.

1 John 3:4. Whoever committeth sin transgresseth also the law: for sin is the transgression of the law.

And there will never be a better definition of sin than this. However men may philosophically try to mar it, this simple statement will be better than any that they can give us: “Sin is the transgression of the law.”

1 John 3:5. And ye know that he was manifested to take away our sins; and in him is no sin.

What a marvellous thing it was for Christ to bear sin as he did, and yet to have upon him or within him no taint arising from it. You have to go into the world, and you say, "How can we help sinning while we have to mix with so much that is evil?" Well, the Lord Jesus Christ had to mix with evil more than you will ever have to do, for he not only lived in this sinful world, but the transgression of his people was actually laid upon him, so that he came into very close contact with sin: "He was manifested to take away our sirs; and in him is no sin."

1 John 3:6. Whoever abideth in him sinneth not: whosoever sinneth hath not seen him, neither known him.

If this declaration related to any one act of sin, none of us could ever say that we have seen or known him, but it relates to the habit of sin, — if we love sin, and live in sin, if the main course of our life is sinful, then we have "not seen him, neither known him."

1 John 3:7. Little children, let no man deceive you: he that doeth righteousness is righteous, even as he is righteous.

You must judge a tree by its fruit; if it brings forth good fruit, it is a good tree, and if it brings forth evil fruit, it is an evil tree. Do not be deceived about that matter, for there have been some, who have dreamed of being righteous, and of being the children of God, yet they have lived in sin as others do. They have been self-deceived; it has been a mere dream on which they have relied. Practical godliness is absolutely needful to a true Christian character, and a man is not righteous unless he does that which is righteous.

1 John 3:8. He that committeth sin is of the devil; for the devil sinneth from the beginning.

Ever since he became a devil, he has continued to sin. It was sin that changed the angel into a devil, and a sinner he has always remained.

1 John 3:8-9. For the purpose the Son of God was manifested; that he might destroy the works of the devil. Whoever is born of God doth not commit sin;

That is to say, this is not the course, and habit, and tenour of his life; there is sin in much that he does, but he hates it, loathes it, and flees from it.

1 John 3:9-11. For his seed remaineth in him: and he cannot sin, because he is born of God. In this the children of God are manifest, and the children of the devil, whosoever doeth not righteousness is not of God, neither he that loveth not his brother. For this is the message that ye heard from the beginning, that we should love one another.

Love is the essential mark of the true child of God. “God is love;” and, therefore, he that is born of God must love. Hatred, envy, malice, uncharitableness, — these are not the things to be found in the children of God; if they are found in you, you are not one of his children.

1 John 3:12. Not as Cain, who was of that wicked one, and slew his brother. And wherefore slew he him? Because his own works were evil, and his brother's righteous.

That was the real evil at the bottom of his great crime; it was the wickedness of Cain's character that made him hate the good that was in Abel; and, therefore, after a while, he slew his brother, “because his own works were evil, and his brother's righteous.”

1 John 3:13. Marvel not, my brethren, if the world hate you.

This hatred is too old for you to wonder at it. If it began with the first man who was born into the world, even with Cain, do not marvel if it should spend some of its fury upon you.

1 John 3:14-15. We know that we have passed from death unto life, because we love the brethren. He that loveth not his brother abideth in death. Whosoever hateth his brother is a murderer: and ye know that no murderer hath eternal life abiding in him.

What a warning this is against the evil spirit of hate, revenge, and all that kind of feeling! These things are not compatible with the possession of the life of God. Where hatred lives, there is no life of God in the soul. That evil must be shot to the very heart, by the arrows of almighty grace, or else we are not free from the dominion of the devil. Every man who hates another has the venom of murder in his veins. He may never actually take the deadly weapons into his hand and destroy life; but if he wishes that his brother were out of the way, if he would be glad if no such person existed, that feeling amounts to murder in the judgment of God. It is not the lifting of the dagger, nor the mixing of the poison, that is the essence of the grime of murder, it is the hate that prompts the commission of the deadly deed; so, if we never commit the crime, yet, if the hate be in our heart, we are guilty of murder in the sight of God, and eternal life cannot be abiding in us.

1 John 3:16-17. Hereby perceive we the love of God, because he laid down his life for us and we ought to lay down our lives for the brethren. But whose hath this world's good, and seeth his brother have need, and shutteth up his bowels of compassion from him, how dwelleth the love of God in him?

Indeed, it cannot be there at all; he has the love of himself, and not the love of God, dwelling in him.

1 John 3:18-19. My little children, let us not love in word, neither in tongue, but in deed and in truth. And hereby we know that we are of the truth, and shall assure our hearts before him.

You notice how the apostle constantly writes about knowing. Take your pencil, and underline the word "know" in John's Epistles, and you will be surprised to find how frequently he uses it. He is not one of those who suppose, or fancy, or imagine, or have formed a certain hypothesis; but he knows, and he tells us what he knows, in order that we also may know. Love hath a knowledge which is peculiarly her own, — a full assurance which none can take from her.

1 John 3:20. For if our heart condemn us, God is greater than our heart, and knoweth all things.

If you, with your narrow knowledge of right and wrong, — your imperfect understanding of your own motives, — if you find reason to condemn yourself, what must be your position before the bar of the all-seeing, heart-reading God? That little flutter in thy bosom, my friend, that trembling, that uneasiness, what means it? It not this a forewarning of the sounding of the trumpet of the great assize, when thou wilt have to stand before the Judge of all the earth, and answer for thyself to him? It is easy to deceive thy fellow-man, but it is impossible to deceive thy God.

1 John 3:21. Beloved, if our heart condemn us not, then have we confidence toward God.

Other people may condemn us, but that does not matter; they may impute to us wrong motives, and misrepresent us, but that is no concern of ours so long as we have confidence toward God.

1 John 3:22. And whatsoever we ask, we receive of him, because we keep his commandments, and do those things that are pleasing in his sight.

Notice the link between confidence as to our rightness and power in prayer. When a child has done wrong, and knows it, he cannot run to his father, and ask for favors as he used to do; he feels timid in his father's presence because of the sense of his guilt. But if you and I know that we have endeavored with all our heart to love the Lord and our fellow-men and to act righteously in all things, we have a saved confidence which enables us to speak with God as a man speaketh with his friend; and this kind of confidence God greatly loves and he listens to those who possess it. Such people may ask what they will of God; they have learned to bring their minds into conformity with the will of God's, so the desire of their heart shall be granted to them.

1 John 3:23-24. And this is his commandment, That we should believe on the name of his Son Jesus Christ, and love one another, as he gave us commandment. And he that keepeth his commandments dwelleth in him, and he in him. And hereby we know that he abideth in us, by the Spirit which he hath given us.

Oh, to be more and more under the saved influence of that blessed Spirit!

Verses 10-24

1 John 3:10-12. In this the children of God are manifest and the children of the devil: whosoever doeth not righteousness is not of God, neither he that loveth not his brother. For this is the message that ye heard from the beginning that we should love one another. Not as Cain, who was of that wicked one, and slew his brother. And wherefore slew he him? Because his own works were evil, and his brother's righteous.

Some people try to deceive us with the notion that all men are the children of God; but John, writing under the inspiration of the Holy Spirit, shows how false that idea is. Holiness and love distinguish the children of God from the children of the devil.

1 John 3:13. Marvel not, my brethren, if the world hate you.

As Cain hated Abel, so worldlings hate the saints, whose holiness is a continual rebuke to the ungodly.

1 John 3:14-16. We know that we have passed from death unto life, because we love the brethren. He that loveth not his brother abideth in death.

Whosoever hateth his brother is a murderer: and ye know that no murderer hath eternal life abiding in him. Hereby perceive we the love of God, because he laid down his life for us: and we ought to lay down our lives for the brethren. Such self-sacrifice as this is the very highest form of love to the brethren, and is a following of the example of Christ, who "laid down his life for us."

1 John 3:17-18. But whoso hath this world's good, and seeth his brother have need and shutteth up his bowels of compassion from him, how dwelleth the love of God in him? My little children, let us not love in word, neither in tongue; but in deed and in truth.

Love that consists only of words is utterly worthless, if it is true love, it must prove itself by kind deeds and gracious actions.

1 John 3:19. And hereby we know that we are of the truth, and shall assure our hearts before him.

The love that will pass this test will bring a restful assurance of peace to the heart.

1 John 3:20-22. For if our heart condemn us, God is greater that our heart, and knoweth all things. Beloved, if our heart condemn us not, then have we confidence toward God. And whatsoever we ask, we receive of him, because we keep his commandments. And do these things that are pleasing in his sight.

It is not everyone who can have whatever he chooses to ask of God in prayer. This privilege is only granted to those who “keep his commandments, and do those things that are pleasing in his sight.”

1 John 3:23. And this is his commandment, That we should believe on the name of his Son Jesus Christ, and love one another, as he gave us commandment.

Faith and love-faith in Christ, and love to one another,-are here most happily joined together; let us never put them asunder.

1 John 3:24. And he that keepeth his commandments dwelleth in him, and he in him. And hereby we know that he abideth in us, by the Spirit which he hath given us.

Though this great truth of our dwelling in God, and God dwelling in us, is a great mystery, it is a mystery concerning which we need not be in doubt if we will learn of the Holy Spirit what he delights to teach us.

SPURGEON 1 JOHN 4

Verses 1-21

1 John 4:1. Beloved, believe not every spirit, —

A simpleton believes every word that he hears, but "the wise man's eyes are in his head," so he examines what he sees and hears, and does not blindly accept whatever may be told to him. So John says, "Believe not every spirit," —

1 John 4:1-3. But try the spirits whether they are of God: because many false prophets are gone out into the world. Hereby know ye the Spirit of God:

Every spirit that confesseth that Jesus Christ is come in the flesh is of God: and every spirit that confesseth not that Jesus Christ is come in the flesh is not of God: If there is any question raised about the Deity and the humanity of Christ, do not listen any longer. When you taste the first morsel of meat from a joint, and you find that it is tainted, there is no necessity for you to eat all the rest to see if it is good; and if any man questions the true Divinity and the real humanity of Christ, have nothing to do with him, and give no heed to what he says, for he "is not of God."

1 John 4:3-4. And this is that spirit of antichrist, whereof ye have heard that it should come; and even now already is it in the world. Ye are of God, little children,

Ye who are trusting in Jesus, and are born again of his Spirit, though you may have only a small influence with others, and are but as little children in your own esteem, yet "ye are of God."

1 John 4:4. And have overcome them: because greater is he that is in you, than he that is in the world.

There are two spirits; the Holy Spirit dwells in believers, and the evil spirit dwells in the ungodly. But the Holy Spirit is stronger than the evil spirit, and will certainly overcome him.

1 John 4:5. They are of the world: therefore speak they of the world, and the world heareth them.

When people say to you, "Everybody says so-and-so," that is not the reason why you should believe it. "All the men of advanced thought, — all the scholars of the age, speak thus;" yes, just so: "They are of the world: therefore speak they of the world, and the world heareth them."

1 John 4:6. We are of God: he that knoweth God heareth us; he that is not of God heareth not us.

The apostles spake as men sent from God, for the Spirit of God dwelt in them; and they alone know the truth who keep to that which has been revealed to us through his holy apostles and prophets.

1 John 4:6-7. Hereby know we the spirit of truth, and the spirit of error. Beloved, let us love one another: for love is of God; and everyone that loveth is born of God, and knoweth God.

From the abundance of love which was in John's heart, we might almost be startled at the very strong things that he writes against those who are in error, did we not remember that it is only a false charity which winks at error. He is the most loving man who has honesty enough to tell the truth, and to speak out boldly against falsehood. It is very easy to pass through this world believing and saying that everybody is right. That is the way to make a soft path for your own feet, and to show that you only have love to yourself; but sometimes to speak as John the Baptist spoke, or as Martin Luther spoke, is the way to prove that you have true love to others.

1 John 4:8-10. He that loveth not knoweth not God; for God is love. In this was manifested the love of God toward us, because that God sent his only begotten Son into the world, that we might live through him. Herein is love, not that we loved God, but that he loved us, and sent his Son to be the propitiation for our sins.

By nature, we had no love to God; we were his enemies. We loved sin, and we had ruined ourselves by it; but God took out of his own bosom the only Son he had, that he might make reconciliation for us, and put away our sin. "Herein is love," says the apostle, as though you could find it nowhere else as it is here. Here is the height and depth of love immeasurable; here is love summed up, here is love's climax: "Herein is love, not that we loved God, but that he loved us, and sent his Son to be the propitiation for our sins."

1 John 4:11. Beloved, if God so loved us, we ought also to love one another.

If such was his great kindness toward us that he denied himself his own Son for our sake, ought we not to be kindly affectioned one toward another?

1 John 4:12. No man hath seen God at any time. If we love one another, God dwelleth in us, and his love is perfected in us.

"God dwelleth in us" though we do not see him. The nearest approach we can have to God is by this golden way of love.

1 John 4:13-14. Hereby know we that we dwell in him, and he in us, because he hath given us of his Spirit. And we have seen and do testify that the Father sent the Son to be the Saviour of the world.

John is speaking for himself and the rest of the apostles; for they were eye-witnesses who had seen Christ, and therefore could testify to him.

1 John 4:15-16. Whosoever shall confess that Jesus is the Son of God, God dwelleth in him, and he in God. And we have known and believed the love that God hath to us. God is love; and he that dwelleth in love dwelleth in God, and God in him.

Is there anyone here who is full of anger, enmity, malice, and envy? If so, let him know that God dwells not in the heart that harbors such abominations. Until these base passions are expelled, and we feel love to all mankind for Christ's sake, God is not in us, for "he that dwelleth in love dwelleth in God, and God in him." The old method, according to Jewish tradition, was, "Thou shalt love thy neighbor, and hate thine enemy;" but Christ's new rule is, "Love your enemies, bless them that curse you, do good to them that hate you, and pray for them which despitefully use you, and persecute you; that ye may be the children of your Father which is in heaven." This is the point in which our likeness to God will be seen, for he loved us when we were his enemies, and he expects his children to love their enemies; may he graciously teach us that sacred art!

1 John 4:17. Herein is our love made perfect, that we may have boldness in the day of judgment: because as he is, so are we in this world.

If we can be to the world, in our poor feeble measure, what God is to it, —fountains of love, dispensaries of goodness, — then we need not be afraid of the verdict even of the great day of judgment.

1 John 4:18. There is no fear in love; but perfect love casteth out fear:

If a man is conscious that he intends no harm to anyone, that he wishes good to all mankind, that he loves his God, and loves his fellowmen for God's sake, what has he to fear? He becomes the bravest of the brave, and often finds himself safe and unharmed in places where others dare not go.

1 John 4:18-20. Because fear hath torment. He that feareth is not made perfect in love. We love him, because he first loved us. If a man say, I love God, and hateth his brother, he is a liar:

John! John! John! This is a very strong expression. Did we not always understand that John was full of affection? Yes, but he was not one of those oily, sugary sort of people who cannot speak the truth. There is no real love in that kind of man; he has only the mere pretense of love. John speaks sharply because he loves ardently. True love hates that which is unlovely. It is inevitable that a man, who is full of love, should feel intense indignation against that which is contrary to love. Hence the apostle says, "If a man say, I love God, and hateth his brother, he is a liar."

1 John 4:20-21. For he that loveth not his brother whom he hath seen, how can he love God whom he hath not seen? And this commandment have we from him, That he who loveth God love his brother also.

And the word "brother" is to be understood in the widest possible sense. We are all brothers, springing from the same common parent; and therefore we ought to be philanthropists, lovers of man, loving even the guilty and the worthless, having an earnest desire to do good even to those who do us ill. If we have not yet reached that spirit, we had need begin our true Christian life, at the foot of the cross, by trusting and loving him who there died out of love for sinners; for there only can we learn, in the person of Christ Jesus our Lord, this divine philosophy of love to God and men.

Verses 9-21

1 John 4:9. In this was manifested the love of God toward us, because that God sent his only begotten Son into the world, that we might live through him.

There is love in our creation; there is love in providence; but most of all there is love in the gift of Christ for our redemption. The apostle here seems to say, "Now that I have found the great secret of God's love to us; here is the clearest evidence of divine love that ever was or ever can be manifested toward the sons of men."

1 John 4:10. Herein is love, not that we loved God, but that he loved us, and sent his Son to be the propitiation for our sins.

In us there was no love; there was a hatred of God and goodness. The enmity was not on God's side toward us; but on our side toward him. "He loved us and sent his son." The gift of Christ; the needful propitiation for our sins, was all of love on God's part. Justice demanded the propitiation, but love applied it. God could not be just if he pardoned sin without atonement; but the greatness of the love is seen in the fact that it moved the Father to give his Son to an ignominious death, that he might pardon sinners and yet be just.

1 John 4:11. Beloved, if God so loved us, we ought also to love one another.

Here we have a fact and an argument. We ought to love. We ought to love after God's fashion; not because men loved us. Nor because they deserve anything at our hands. We are too apt to look at the worthiness of those whom we help; but our God is gracious to the unthankful and to the evil.
He makes his sun to rise and rain to fall for the unjust as well as for the righteous, therefore we ought to love the unlovely and the unloving. But just as God has a special love for his own people, we who believe in him ought to have a peculiar affection for all who are his.

1 John 4:12. No man hath seen God at any time.

We do not need to see him to love him. Love knows how good he is, though she hath not beheld him. Blessed are they who have not seen God, yet who love him with heart, and mind, and strength.

1 John 4:12. If we love one another, God dwelleth in us, and his love is perfected in us.

He is not far to seek. If you love one another, God is in you; he dwells in you, he is your nearest and dearest Friend, the Author of all other love. The grace of love comes from the God of love.

1 John 4:13. Hereby know we that we dwell in him, and he in us, because he hath given us of his Spirit.

And his Spirit is the spirit of love. Wherever it comes, it makes man love his fellow man and seek his good; and if you have that love in your heart, it came from God, and you dwell in God.

1 John 4:14. And we have seen.

Yes, there is something that we have seen. John writes for himself and his fellow apostles, and he says, "No man hath seen God at any time," but —

1 John 4:14. We have seen and do testify that the Father sent the Son to be the Saviour of the world.

John saw him live, and saw him die, and saw him when he had risen from the dead, and saw him as he ascended. So he speaks to the matter of eyesight, and bears testimony that, though we have not seen God, we have, in the person of the representative apostles, seen the Son of God who lived and laboured and died for us.

1 John 4:15. Whosoever shall confess that Jesus is the Son of God, God dwelleth in him, and he in God.

Let Christ be God to you, and you are saved. If, in every deed, and of a truth. You take him to be the Son of God, and consequently rest your eternal hopes on him, God dwells in you, and you dwell in God.

1 John 4:16. And we have known and believed the love that God hath to us.

How far is this true of all of you? How many here can join with the beloved apostle, and say, "We have known and believed the love that God hath to us"? We know it; we have felt it; we are under its power. We know it still, it remains a matter of faith to us; we believe it. We have a double hold of it. "We know," we are not agnostics. "We believe," we are not unbelievers.

1 John 4:16. God is love; and he that dwelleth in love dwelleth in God, and God in him.

This is not mere benevolence; there are many benevolent people who still do not dwell in love. They wish well to their fellow men; but not to all. They are full of indignation at certain men for the wrong that they have done them. John's words teach us that there is a way of living in which you are in accord with God, and with all mankind; you have passed out of the region of enmity into the realm of love. When you have come there, by the grace of God, then God dwells in you, and you dwell in him.

1 John 4:17. Herein is our love made perfect, that we may have a boldness in the day of judgment:

That is a wonderful expression, "boldness in the day of judgment." According to some, the saints will not be in the day of judgment. Then, what is the use of "boldness in the day of judgment"? As I read my Bible, we shall all be there, and we shall all give an account unto God. I shall be glad to be there, to be judged for the deeds done in my body; not that I hope to be saved by them, but because I shall have a perfect answer to all accusations on account of my sin. "Who is he that condemneth? It is Christ that died, yea, rather, that is risen again, who is even at the right hand of God, who also maketh intercession for us." If I am a believer in Christ, —

"Bold shall I stand in that grand day,
For who aught to my charge shall lay?
While through thy blood absolved I am From sin's tremendous curse and shame."
Because as he is, so are we in this world.

Happy Christian men, who can say that? If you live among men as Christ lived among men, if you are a Saviour to them in your measure, if you love them, if you try to exhibit the lovely traits of character that were in Christ, happy are you.

1 John 4:18. There is no fear in love;

When a man loves with a perfect love, he escapes from bondage.

1 John 4:18. But perfect love casteth out fear: because fear hath torment. He that feareth is not made perfect in love.

There is a loving, holy fear, which is never cast out. Filial fear grows as love grows. That sacred dread, that solemn awe of God, we must ever cultivate; but we are not afraid of him. Dear heart, God is your best Friend, your choicest love. "Yea, mine own God is he," you can say; and you have no fear of him now. You long to approach him. Though he is a consuming fire, you know that he will only consume what you want to have consumed; and will purify you, and make your gold to shine more brightly because the consumable alloy is gone from it. He will not consume you, but only that which would work for your hurt if it were left within you. Refining fire, go through my heart! Consume as thou wilt! I long to have sin consumed, that I may be like my God. Say you not so, my brethren?

1 John 4:19. We love him, because he first loved us.

The reason for our love is found in free grace. God first loved us, and now we must love him; we cannot help it. It sometimes seems too much for a poor sinner to talk about loving God. If an emmet or a snail were to say that it loved a queen, you would think it strange, that it should look so high for an object of affection; but there is no distance between an insect and a man compared with the distance between man and God. Yet love doth fling a flying bridge from our manhood up to his Godhead. "We love him, because he first loved us." If he could come down to us, we can go up to him. If his love could come down to such unworthy creatures as we are, then our poor love can find wings with which to mount up to him.

1 John 4:20. If a man say, I love God.

Not, "if a man love God," but if a man say, "I love God." It is a blessed thing to be able to say, "I love God," when God himself can bear witness to the truth of our statement; but the apostle says, If a man say, I love God, —

1 John 4:20. And hateth his brother, he is a liar:

It is very rude of you, John, to call people liars. But it is not John's rough nature that uses such strong language; it is his gentle nature. When a loving disposition turns its face against evil, it turns against it with great vehemence of holy indignation. You can never judge a man's character by his books. Curiously enough, Mr. Romaine. Of St. Anne's Church, Blackfriars, wrote the most loving books that could be; yet he was a man of very strong temper indeed. Mr. Toplady wrote some of the sharpest things that were ever said about Arminians; but he was the most loving and gentle young man that ever breathed. St. John, full of love and tenderness, hits terribly hard when he comes across a lie. He was so fond of love, that he cannot have it played with, or mocked or mimicked. "If a man say, I love God, and hateth his brother, he is a liar."

1 John 4:21. For he that loveth not his brother whom he hath seen, how can he love God whom he hath not seen? And this commandment have we from him, That he who loveth God love his brother also.

This is that “new commandment” which our Lord gave to his apostles, and through them to his whole church. “That ye love one another as I have loved you.” John was, in a special sense, “that disciple whom Jesus loved.” It was meet, therefore, that he should be the apostle to be inspired by the Holy Spirit to bring “this commandment” to the remembrance of any who had forgotten it. “This commandment have we from him, That he who loveth God love his brother also.” God help us so to do, of his great grace!

Amen.

SPURGEON 1 JOHN 5

Verses 1-21

1 John 5:1. Whosoever believeth that Jesus is the Christ is born of God.

Take comfort, believer, from that declaration. You have accepted Jesus as the Christ the anointed of God, so the apostle affirms that you are "born of God." It may be only lately that you have been born again, you may be only a babe in grace; but if you have a true faith in Christ as God's anointed, you are "born of God."

1 John 5:1. And every one that loveth him that begat loveth him also that is begotten of him.

If you truly love God, you also love his well-beloved and only-begotten Son, and you also love all his children. There cannot be a true love to the Father and a hatred to his family, that is impossible. Judge therefore by this test whether you love God or not.

1 John 5:2-3. By this we know that we love the children of God, when we love God, and keep his commandments. For this is the love of God, that we keep his commandments and his commandments are not grievous.

Love is a practical thing; love without obedience is a mere pretense. True love shows itself by seeking to please the one who is loved. May God the Holy Ghost work in us perfect obedience to the commands of God, that we may prove that we really do love him!

1 John 5:4. For whatsoever is born of God overcometh the world: and this is the victory that overcometh the world, even our faith.

This is the conquering weapon; he who truly believes in Jesus cannot be overthrown by the combined forces of the world, the flesh, and the devil. Remember the lesson that Haman learned when he contended in vain against Mordecai because Mordecai was of the seed of the Jews, and learn that they who belong to Christ shall, like Christ be more than conquerors.

1 John 5:5. Who is he that overcometh the world, but he that believeth that Jesus the Son of God?

Let that truth be firmly fixed in your mind, and nerve you in your conflict with the world. The old cry, Athanasius contra mundum, "Athanasius against the world," may be uttered by every believer in Jesus into Christianus contra mundum." Who is he that overcometh the world, but he that believeth that Jesus is the Son of God?"

1 John 5:6-7. This is he that came by water and blood, even Jesus Christ, not by water only, but by water and blood. And it is the Spirit that beareth witness, because the Spirit is truth. For there are three that bear record in heaven, the Father, the Word, and the Holy Ghost: and these three are one.

Thus all the Persons in the blessed Trinity confirm the faith of the Christian; the Father, the Son, and the Holy Ghost bear united witness to the faith which God himself gives us.

1 John 5:8. And there are three that bear witness in earth, the Spirit, and the water, and the blood: and these three agree in one.

Three candles in the room, but the light is one, three witnesses to our heart, but the witness is the same. If we have the witness of the Spirit, the water, and the blood, we know that we have received the truth.

1 John 5:9-10. If we receive the witness of men, the witness of God is greater: for this is the witness of God which he hath testified of his Son. He that believeth on the Son of God hath the witness in himself:

What better witness than this could he have?

1 John 5:10. Because he believeth not God hath made him a liar;"-

He need not actually say that God is a liar; the fact that he does no believe him has practically made out that God is a liar. How many of us are there to whom this passage applies?" He that believeth not God hath made him a liar;"-

1 John 5:10. Because he believeth not the record that God gave of his Son.

Is this true concerning anyone here! If so, perhaps if you have not been aware of the extent of your guilt. You have remained unbelievers out of sheer carelessness, out of neglect of the Word. I pray you, rest not in such a state of mind and heart now that you are informed by the Spirit of God that, by your unbelief, you are making God a liar. Who would willfully commit that great sin? Let us shudder at the thought of the bare possibility of such guilt as this.

1 John 5:11. And this is the record, that God hath given to us eternal life, and this life is in his Son.

Our only hope lies in Christ; but there is life for Us in Christ and life eternal, if we do but believe in him.

1 John 5:12. He that hath the Son hath life; and he that hath not the Son of God hath not life.

You exist, and you always will exist, but true life is not yours if you have not Christ as your Saviour. Life is something infinitely superior to mere existence: "He that hath the Son hath life; and he that hath not the Son of God hath not life."

1 John 5:13-15. These things have I written unto you that believe on the name of the Son of God; that ye may know that ye have eternal life, and that ye may believe on the name of the Son of God. And this is the confidence that we have in him, that, if we ask any thing according to his will, he heareth us: and if we know that he hear us, whatsoever we ask, we knew that we have the petitions that we desired of him.

A very wonderful thing is prayer, yet it is not every man's prayer that is heard, but he that hath the life of God within him shall have his petitions granted because the Holy Spirit will move him to ask in accordance with the will of God.

1 John 5:16-18. If any man see his brother sin a sin which is not unto death, he shall ask, and he shall give him life for them that sin not unto death. There is a sin unto death: I do not say that he shall pray for it. All unrighteousness is sin: and there is a sin not unto death. We know that whatsoever is born of God sinneth not; but he that is begotten of God keepeth himself, and that wicked one toucheth him not.

He who has committed the sin which is unto death have no desire for forgiveness, he will never repent, he will never seek faith in Christ but he will continue hardened and unbelieving; he will henceforth never be the subject of holy influences, for he has crossed over into that dark region of despair where hope and mercy never come. Perhaps some of you think that you have committed that unpardonable sin, and are at this moment grieving over it. If so, it is clear that you cannot have committed that sin, or else you could not grieve over it. If you have any fear concerning it, you have not committed that sin which is unto death, for even fear is a sign of life. Whoever repents of sin and trusts in Jesus Christ is freely and fully forgiven, therefore it is clear that he has not committed a sin which will not be forgiven. There is much in this passage to make us prayerful and watchful, but there is nothing here to make a single troubled heart feel anything like despair. He that is born again, born from above, can never commit this unpardonable sin. He is kept from it; "that wicked one" cannot even touch him, for he is preserved by sovereign grace against this dreadful damage to his soul. You need not be curious to enquire what this unpardonable sin is. I will give you an old illustration of mine concerning it.

You may sometimes have seen a notice put up on certain estates in the country, "Man-traps and spring guns set here," but, if so, did you ever go round to the front door of the mansion, and say, "If you please will you tell me where the man-traps are, and whereabouts the spring guns are set?" If you had asked that question, the answer would have been, "It is the very purpose of this warning not to tell you where they are, for you have no business to trespass there at all." So, "all unrighteousness is sin," and you are warned to keep clear of it." There is a sin unto death," but you are not told what that sin is on purpose that you may, by the grace of God, keep clear of sin altogether.

1 John 5:19-21. And we know that we are of God, and the whole world lieth in wickedness. And we know that the Son of God is come, and hath given us an understanding, that we may know him that is true, and we are in him that true, even in his Son Jesus Christ. This is the true God, and eternal life. Little children keep yourselves from idols. Amen.

After the Reformation in England, there was a certain part of the church, called the rood-loft, where the crucifix had to be, and it was ordered by the Reformers, when "the holy rood" was taken away, that these words should be printed in capital letters in its place,-" LITTLE CHILDREN KEEP YOURSELVES FROM IDOLS." This was an admirable arrangement, and this text might very profitably be put up in a good many Ritualistic churches now, instead of the Agnus Dei and the crucifix,-"Little children, keep yourselves from idols." Might we not also say to many a mother and many a father concerning their children, and to many a lover of money and hungerer after gold, "Keep yourselves from idols"? Idolatry will intrude itself in one form or another. Some idolize themselves; they look in the glass, and there see the face of their god. O beware of all idolatry!" Little children, keep yourselves from idols. Amen." We may very well say "Amen" to that.

THANK YOU

Thank you for purchasing this book. We truly value your custom. This book was put together to provide you with a collection of good commentary resources on the books of the Bible. It is our prayerful hope that God might use this work for His own glory and sovereign will.

We would be delighted to hear from you and received any messages, suggestions or corrections. You can contact us at:

expansivecommentarycollection@gmail.com

It is our promise that you email address will not be added to any mailing list or used for any purpose other than to communicate regarding this commentary series.

We trust that the Lord will continue to bless you as you live for Him.

Made in the USA
Middletown, DE
17 September 2022

10670738R00029